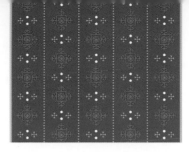

Classic Recipes of
TUSCANY

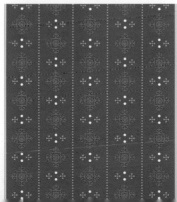

Classic Recipes of
TUSCANY

TRADITIONAL FOOD AND COOKING
IN 25 AUTHENTIC DISHES

VALENTINA HARRIS

LORENZ BOOKS

This edition is published by
Lorenz Books,
an imprint of Anness Publishing Ltd,
108 Great Russell Street,
London WC1B 3NA
info@anness.com
www.annesspublishing.com
twitter: @Anness_Books

© Anness Publishing Limited 2015

If you like the images in this book and
would like to investigate using them for
publishing, promotions or advertising,
please visit our website
www.practicalpictures.com for more
information.

Publisher: Joanna Lorenz
Editor: Helen Sudell
Designer: Nigel Partridge
Recipe Photography: Martin Brigdale
Food Stylist: Valentina Harris
Prop Stylist: Helen Trent
Production Controller: Pirong Wang

A CIP catalogue record for this book is
available from the British Library

PUBLISHER'S NOTE
Although the advice and information in this
book are believed to be accurate and true
at the time of going to press, neither the
authors nor the publisher can accept any
legal responsibility or liability for any errors
or omissions that may have been made nor
for any inaccuracies nor for any loss, harm
or injury that comes about from following
instructions or advice in this book.

PUBLISHER'S ACKNOWLEDGMENTS
The Publisher would like to thank the
following agencies for the use of their
images. Fotalia p6, p10bl. Alamy: p11
(both).

COOK'S NOTES
Bracketed terms are intended for American
readers. For all recipes, quantities are given
in both metric and imperial measures and,
where appropriate, in standard cups and
spoons. Follow one set of measures, but
not a mixture, because they are not
interchangeable.

Standard spoon and cup measures are
level. 1 tsp = 5ml, 1 tbsp = 15ml, 1 cup =
250ml/8fl oz. Australian standard
tablespoons are 20ml. Australian readers
should use 3 tsp in place of 1 tbsp for
measuring small quantities.

American pints are 16fl oz/2 cups.
American readers should use 20fl oz/2.5
cups in place of 1 pint when measuring
liquids.

Electric oven temperatures in this book are
for conventional ovens. When using a fan
oven, the temperature will probably need to
be reduced by about 10–20ºC/20–40ºF.
Since ovens vary, you should check with
your manufacturer's instruction book for
guidance.

The nutritional analysis given for each
recipe is calculated per portion (i.e. serving
or item), unless otherwise stated. If the
recipe gives a range, such as Serves 4–6,
then the nutritional analysis will be for the
smaller portion size, i.e. 6 servings. The
analysis does not include optional
ingredients, such as salt added to taste.

Contents

Introduction

Tuscany is blessed with exceptional beauty and has long been one of Italy's most loved regions. It stretches along the north-western coast of Italy, bound inland by mountains to the north and east. The temperate climate and fertile landscape mean that a diverse range of foods are produced here. As with other parts of Italy, Tuscan cooks have a great respect for all the different elements that make their cuisine unique, and delight in promoting local dishes and ingredients. Recipes that derive from both medieval kitchens and Renaissance banquets have survived the passage of time and are still found today, perhaps with minor adaptations, in the restaurants and homes of Tuscany.

Left: Il Duomo dominates the red-tiled roofs of Florence, the capital of Tuscany.

Tuscan Food and Cooking

The cuisine of Tuscany has been shaped by two distinct groups: recipes that were historically created for the wealthy, and another set of recipes cooked by the poor. Only the nobility or the clergy would have been able to afford expensive ingredients such as salt, sugar, fine flour or spices. Peasant farmers would have lived off different fare, eating a more repetitive, basic diet. Both types of cooking survive today, although it is the simpler peasant dishes that have defined the traditional cuisine of Tuscany most clearly.

Below: The fish soup cacciucco is made throughout Tuscany but originates from Livorno.

Above: Tuscans love to dunk the hard biscuits, cantucci, in dessert wine.

Tuscan Cuisine

Fragrant local olive oil is chosen as the main cooking fat over more expensive options of butter or pork fat. Along the coast, full use has always been made of the daily fish and shellfish catch, with the port city of Livorno leading the way with its famous fish soup, *cacciucco*.

Next to olive oil, bread is the most fundamental part of Tuscan cuisine. Different breads are made all over the region and come in a multitude of types and flavours: long, flattish loaves, unsalted bread, crown-shaped loaves, crostini, or the Florentine *schiacciata all'uva*, which is prepared only during the grape harvest.

Local Specialities

Many of the region's towns are known for specific dishes. Florence has the huge Fiorentina steak; nearby Prato is where the much-loved dunking biscuits, *cantucci*, were created. Pisa is dominated by the truffles of nearby San Miniato, as well as locally caught eels and a dried salted cod, or *stoccafisso*.

In the Maremma, a flat marshy land, the most celebrated local dish is named *acquacotta*, 'cooked water'. This simple dish would originally have been made with nothing more than bread, water and a little olive oil, with a sprinkling of the sharp local Pecorino cheese, although nowadays a number of other ingredients are added as toppings.

Right: Home-made bread is central to the traditional Tuscan meal and comes in many forms.

Tuscan Festivals

Italians love an excuse for a party. As well as an array of religious celebrations, there is a vast number of small local festivals that take place across the country.

Christmas

All over Italy, the solemn rituals of Christmas Eve (*Vigilia* – keeping watch) are celebrated. The traditional Vigilia feast features seven dishes to represent the seven sacraments, with simple pasta dishes that do not contain any meat, at least

Below: Befana witches on sale at a Christmas market, Pisa.

until after the celebration of the midnight Mass. A light meal is eaten before the Mass, followed by a huge celebratory feast, featuring fresh pasta, roasted meat, guinea fowl, and cakes and pastries. After all this feasting, Christmas Day and St Stephen's Day (Boxing Day) tend to be much quieter days, largely devoted to visiting family and friends.

Epiphany

Traditionally, Epiphany is the day when gifts are exchanged. La Befana, the warty old witch, comes to visit children on her broomstick, bringing presents for those that have been good and a lump of coal for those who have been naughty. Special cakes are prepared in honour of this day, sometimes baked in the embers of the fire for Befana to find when she comes down the chimney.

Carnival

The most important day of Carnival is *Martedi Grasso*, the last day before Ash Wednesday,

Above: Deep-fried pastry strips are popular during Carnival.

which marks the beginning of Lent and the long quiet period of self-denial. Martedi Grasso (Fat Tuesday) is a day of feasting, a final thrilling moment of pure indulgence before Lent. During Carnival, the custom is to fry great batches of sweet *sfrappé*, simple sugared pastry strips flavoured with a little wine.

Easter

In the past, meat was never eaten on Good Friday. Although this is no longer an official Church rule, it is still respected by some religious households. So fish and vegetables, usually simply cooked, are served on this day, which for many is a time of quiet reflection.

In some homes a variety of flat omelettes, called frittatas, along with an assortment of sausages and other meats, are served on Holy Saturday with *pane di Pasqua* or Easter bread. Easter Sunday is celebrated with special breads and pastries, as well as the main Easter feast, with the *agnello Pasquale* (Easter lamb) as the centrepiece of the meal.

Below: Paschal bread is eaten on Easter Sunday.

One of the most joyous of Italian traditions, *Pasquetta* (Easter Monday), is the unofficial start of spring and a chance to get reacquainted with loved-ones and the great outdoors. Families and friends go out in droves to the mountains or the beaches and set up camp to have large picnics. They eat frittatas (omelettes) or hard-boiled eggs and an assortment of grilled meats.

Fritelle Festival

This festival takes place in the beautiful walled village of Monteflorälle on the Sunday following St Joseph's Day in March. Hundreds of *Fritelle*, fried rice cakes, are made in a cauldron of oil and everyone shares them out.

Porcino Festival

The most famous Italian mushroom is celebrated in the town of Ronta in Tuscany at the end of the summer, where an entire menu based on porcini mushrooms is cooked and eaten with great relish.

Above: A flag waver of the Onda at the Palio dc Siena, a twice-yearly event of pageantry and horse racing.

The Palio

This famous horse race occurs twice a year in Siena, Tuscany on the 2nd July and 16th August. Ten horse riders, representing the *contrades*, or districts, of Siena compete in the race. The festivities begin three days prior to the horse race, however, with banquets and colourful parades for each contrade competing.

Classic Ingredients

The key to all Italian cooking is quality fresh ingredients. From fish, meats and cheeses to fruit, vegetables and beans, they are crucial to good taste.

Fish and Shellfish

The Tuscan coastline has a good supply of all kinds of fish and shellfish from the Mediterranean sea, but freshwater fish also appears on the region's menus. The Italian tradition of eating salted cod (*baccalà*) persists from the time when cod had to be preserved in this way on its long journey to Italy from the North Sea fishing grounds. The dry, salty fish pieces are soaked well before being used in recipes, including tasty fritters, for which the fish is coated in batter and fried.

Game

Wild boar are hunted in Tuscany every autumn and are then used to make a traditional rich stew with tomatoes and red wine, known as *cinghiale alla cacciatora*. Wild boar meat also goes into creating strong, flavourful sausages, which provide hearty winter fare for the colder months.

Rabbit and guinea fowl are also popular game meats, and at Christmas time, most Central Italians prefer to eat capons, rather than a turkey.

Meat

Perhaps the most typical and woll-known meat recipe of Tuscany is the huge, tender steak known as *la Fiorentina*. This mouthwatering piece of meat is served grilled (broiled) with a little oil, rosemary, salt, and sometimes garlic.

In rural areas, the coming of winter means the slaughter of the family pig, which provides cured meat, sausages and pork fat to last throughout the cold winter weather. *Lardo di Colonnata* (cured pork fat) is a famous Tuscan speciality, which is served thinly sliced and then laid over a warm slice of toasted polenta or bread.

Dairy Produce

Tuscans love a sharp and tasty sheep's cheese, such as Pecorino, and many kinds are produced throughout the region. Grated Parmesan cheese is sprinkled over pasta and other dishes, and soft ricotta is ideal for a tasty dessert or mixed into a savoury pasta filling. Butter and milk are the principal ingredients in béchamel or white sauce, which Italians claim was invented by Medici cooks who took it to France sometime during the 16th century.

Below: The Tuscan coastline ensures an ample supply of fish.

Right: Finely grated Parmesan cheese is an integral part of many pasta dishes.

Above: Grapes are eaten fresh and also in some Tuscan meals.

Fruit and Nuts

Citrus fruits appear on the market stalls all over Italy in the winter. Oranges and tangerines tend to be eaten fresh while lemons are an important ingredient for many dishes, both sweet and savoury. Lemon juice is a popular dressing for vegetables: it is drizzled along with good-quality olive oil over freshly steamed greens or other vegetables. Grapes, red and green, are not only made into beautiful wines, but also eaten fresh or used as a special topping for harvest bread or to accompany the region's rich, meaty sausages.

The sweet chestnut season starts in late October, and chestnut flour is used to make a cake called *castagnaccio*. Almonds are used in a host of traditional desserts and cakes.

Vegetables

Fresh vegetables are an essential part of the Tuscan cook's resources and typical vegetables of the region feature across the menu.

Cavolo nero (black cabbage) is harvested during the winter and early spring. It is eaten braised, or as a nourishing ingredient in hearty soups such as the classic ribollita. Onions and garlic are fundamental ingredients for virtually all savoury dishes.

Spring brings the new artichokes, beginning with the smaller varieties, which have a unique, strong flavour that blends well with pasta. Fresh beans and peas also mark the start of the spring season.

In high summer, a huge variety of different kinds of courgette (zucchini) are grown.

Above: Tomatoes grown in Tuscany are sweet and juicy.

They are especially tasty when cut into little batons, dipped in batter and deep-fried. Summers in Tuscany are hot enough to produce a good crop of sweet tomatoes, which are used in cooking and also eaten fresh in salads.

In autumn, mushrooms are gathered fresh from the fields, then either eaten straight away or dried and reconstituted later to add their strong flavour to pasta dishes, stews or soups. Truffles are a favourite but expensive delicacy – tiny shavings are often added to a plain omelette, where their flavour really shines through.

Above: Olives and olive oil are used daily in Tuscan cuisine.

Olives grow everywhere in these regions, freshly picked in autumn to be marinated, or pressed to make the most delicious olive oil.

Pulses

Tuscans are known throughout Italy as the *mangiafagioli* (bean eaters), due to their unsurpassed passion for beans of all kinds. They eat them in salads and cook them in soups and stews, both fresh when available and dried. The most famous and highly valued lentils in Italy come from the area around Castelluccio in Umbria and are pale brown, and small in size.

Grains, Polenta and Pasta

Bread is a vital ingredient in many dishes. In Tuscany, to make a simple soup more substantial and filling, lightly toasted slices of bread are used to line the bowl before the soup is poured over.

Polenta flour is used to make cakes or can be added to wheat flour for specific kinds of bread. Spelt is another grain that makes tasty, gluten-free bread, as well as a nutritious stew or soup, mixed with plenty of fresh vegetables.

Tuscan pasta includes *pappardelle*, thumb-wide egg pasta ribbons, often served with

Below: Dried or fresh beans feature in many Tuscan recipes.

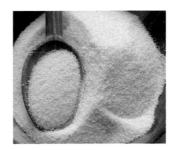

Above: Polenta can often constitute a meal in itself.

a hare sauce; unevenly cut rectangles of egg pasta known as *maltagliati*; and *pici*, irregular strands of flour-and-water pasta, which is slightly thicker than spaghetti.

Herbs

Rosemary is the symbolic taste and perfume of Tuscany. Even the humblest of dishes use this wonderfully fragrant herb to enhance their flavour. Other favourites include basil, sage, and flat leaf parsley. Fiery red chilli peppers feature in some meat and fish dishes, and juniper berries are often added to a rich wild boar stew.

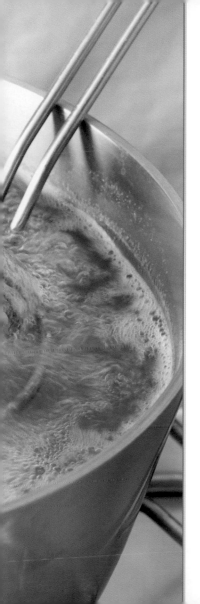

Tuscan Delights

Most Italian dishes are actually very simple and focus on just a few fundamental elements – this could be a piece of meat from the local butcher, a tender home-grown vegetable picked from the garden, or some delicate pasta made that morning at the kitchen table. From hearty soups such as Tuscan Bean and Cabbage Soup to comforting Spinach Gnocchi, and from the classic Tuscan Fish Stew to a rich Wild Boar Cacciatora, as well as irresistible cakes and bakes like Panforte and the seasonal Grape Focaccia, the recipes presented here offer an insight into the very best of Tuscany's wonderful culinary heritage.

Left: Cooking fresh gnocchi is an essential skill for any Italian cook.

Tuscan Cold Summer Soup Zuppa dei Mori

Serves 6

½ cucumber, peeled and cubed
1 fennel bulb, thinly sliced
1 celery heart, chopped
1 lettuce, chopped
4 tomatoes, peeled, seeded and
    chopped
3 carrots, quartered
1 lemon, peeled and thinly sliced
3 garlic cloves, chopped
1 dried red chilli, finely chopped
1 bunch fresh basil
75ml/2½fl oz/⅓ cup extra virgin
    olive oil
sea salt and ground black pepper
croûtons, to serve (optional)

The origins of this cold soup date back to the Medici court, and it is believed to have been created for banquets honouring guests from North Africa, hence the name Mori, which translates as Moors. Cooling and delicious, this soup is perfect for serving on hot summer days.

1 Place the cucumber, slices of fennel, chopped celery, lettuce, tomatoes, carrots, lemon, garlic, chilli and basil in the bowl of a food processor, and gradually process all ingredients until well mixed; alternatively, use a blender and blend until smooth.

2 Add 250ml/8fl oz/1 cup water and the extra virgin olive oil, then season with salt and black pepper to taste.

3 Ladle into a serving bowl and chill until required. Serve with croûtons, if you like.

COOK'S TIP
To peel tomatoes, place in a bowl, cover with boiling water and leave for 30 seconds. Refresh under cold water, score a cross at the bottom of the tomato and the skins will peel off easily.

Tomato and Bread Soup Pappa al Pomodoro

Serves 6

1.5 litres/2½ pints/6¼ cups
   vegetable, chicken or meat stock
1 large onion, chopped
1.2kg/2½lb very ripe tomatoes,
   coarsely chopped
120ml/4fl oz/½ cup extra virgin
   olive oil
400g/14oz stale ciabatta, crusts
   removed, thinly sliced
3 garlic cloves, crushed
a large handful of fresh basil leaves,
   chopped
sea salt and ground black pepper

This is a very thick, almost solid, soup, which makes the best of the glut of overripe tomatoes at the end of a Tuscan summer. These are combined with that ever-present standby ingredient: stale bread. It is marvellous served lukewarm with plenty of basil and extra olive oil to drizzle over it.

1 Heat the stock gently in a large pan. Meanwhile, put the onion, tomatoes and half the oil in a separate pan and fry together over a gentle heat for 10 minutes, or until softened.

2 Push the onion and tomato mixture through a food mill or sieve (strainer) and add it to the hot stock. Stir thoroughly.

3 Add the bread, garlic and most of the basil, and season to taste.

4 Cover and simmer gently for 45 minutes, or until thick and creamy, stirring occasionally. Stir in the remaining oil, adjust the seasoning, and add the rest of the basil to taste. Serve hot or at room temperature.

COOK'S TIP

Pushing the soup through a food mill (a mouli) or a wide-meshed sieve or strainer is essential to get the right texture. Do not be tempted to blitz it in a food processor, or it will be too smooth.

Serves 4 to 6

250g/9oz stale country-style white or
  brown bread, sliced
30ml/2 tbsp olive oil, plus extra to
  serve
3 carrots, coarsely chopped
2 potatoes, peeled and cubed
2 garlic cloves, finely chopped
2 onions, finely sliced
1 small cabbage, shredded
2–3 handfuls of any other leaf
  vegetables of your choice, such as
  spinach or chard, coarsely
  shredded
4 Italian pork or wild boar sausages
about 1.2 litres/2 pints/5 cups cold
  water
150g/5oz/1 cup cooked cannellini
  beans (see Cook's Tips)
sea salt and ground black pepper
freshly grated Parmesan or Pecorino
  cheese, to serve (optional)

Tuscan Bean, Sausage and Cabbage Soup La Ribollita

1 Season the stale bread with salt and pepper. Brush it thoroughly on either side with the olive oil. Use the bread to line a soup tureen or large heatproof bowl.

2 Put all the vegetables and the sausages into a large pan and cover with the cold water. Season with salt and pepper and cover with a lid. Bring to the boil, then reduce the heat and simmer for 1½ hours, stirring occasionally and adding water if the liquid reduces too much.

3 Remove the sausages and keep warm. Stir the beans into the soup and simmer for a further 10 minutes.

4 Adjust the seasoning to taste, then pour the soup over the prepared bread in the tureen or bowl. Arrange the sausages on top, then cover and leave to rest for about 10 minutes before serving. Serve with a jug or pitcher of olive oil to drizzle over the soup, and Parmesan or Pecorino cheese, if you like.

COOK'S TIPS
• Very stale bread is best for this recipe.
• If using canned beans, rinse them thoroughly before using. If using dried beans, soak 50g/ 2oz/⅓ cup overnight in cold water, then rinse. Boil them for 5 minutes, drain and rinse. Return to the pan with fresh water. Boil gently until tender.

An absolutely classic Tuscan recipe, la ribollita is typical of the big, wholesome soups of this region. At the table, offer around olive oil so that people can drizzle it over their individual portions – this is known as blessing your soup. You can also offer grated Parmesan or Pecorino cheese.

Tuscan Bread Fritters Ficattole

Serves 4

300g/11oz/2⅔ cups plain (all-purpose) flour, plus extra for dusting
30g/1¼oz fresh yeast
120ml/4fl oz/½ cup warm water
300ml/½ pint/1¼ cups cold water
olive oil and sunflower oil mixed, for deep-frying (see Cook's Tip)
sea salt

1 Put the flour on to the work surface in a mound and make a hollow in the centre with your fist.

2 Mix the yeast with the warm water and a pinch of salt and stir until dissolved. Work the yeast mixture into the flour, adding enough of the cold water to produce a smooth dough.

3 Knead for 10 minutes, or until soft and spongy. Put the ball of dough into a lightly oiled bowl and cover with oiled clear film (plastic wrap). Leave to rise in a warm place for about 1 hour, or until it has doubled in size.

4 Knock back (punch down) the dough and roll it out on a floured surface. Cut into finger-sized strips.

5 Heat the olive and sunflower oils in a deep-fryer or large, deep pan until a small piece of dough, dropped into the oil, sizzles instantly.

6 Fry the fritters, in batches, for 2–3 minutes, or until golden brown.

7 Remove the fritters carefully from the oil using a slotted spoon. Drain the fritters on kitchen paper and sprinkle with salt. Serve immediately.

COOK'S TIP
Do make sure the oil is really hot before you start to deep-fry the fritters.

These simple and delicious little bread-dough fritters appear all over Tuscany under various different names, but the basic principle is always the same: just flour, salt, water and yeast are needed to make them, and plenty of hot olive oil for deep-frying them until they are crispy and golden brown. Perfect as a little snack, they are usually served with an antipasto platter as an alternative to ordinary bread.

Tuscan Liver Pâté Crostini

Serves 4

45ml/3 tbsp olive oil
40g/1½oz unsalted butter
½ onion, finely chopped
1 carrot, finely chopped
1 celery stick, finely chopped
15ml/1 tbsp finely chopped parsley
1 chicken liver, trimmed
115g/4oz calf's liver, trimmed
30ml/2 tbsp dry white wine
25ml/1½ tbsp tomato purée (paste),
    diluted in 60ml/4 tbsp hot water
25g/1oz salted capers, rinsed and
    finely chopped
4 large or 8 small thin slices crusty
    white or brown bread
sea salt and ground black pepper

*Some say that this is the
original 15th-century recipe
for pâté from the Medici
kitchens. It is a delicious
way to sharpen the appetite
at the start of a meal. In
Tuscany the word crostini
traditionally refers to this
pâté, as opposed to toasted
bread with various toppings.*

1 Put the olive oil and half the butter in a large pan and fry the vegetables over a medium heat for 15 minutes, or until soft.

2 Add the parsley and chicken and calf's livers. Stir well and add the dry white wine. Cook for 2 minutes, stirring constantly, then add the diluted tomato purée.

3 Season to taste, then add 30ml/2 tbsp water, cover and simmer for about 20 minutes.

4 Remove from the heat, lift the livers out of the sauce and chop finely or process them in a food processor or blender until quite smooth.

5 Return the semi-puréed livers to the pan. Stir in the remaining butter and the capers. Heat through and remove from the heat, but keep warm.

6 Spread the bread generously with the liver topping and serve.

Tuscan Bread and Tomato Salad La Panzanella

Serves 4

8 slices casareccio-type bread
   or ciabatta, stale
4 beefsteak tomatoes, chopped
1 large red onion, chopped
1 large cucumber, chopped
a handful of fresh basil leaves,
   torn into pieces
extra virgin olive oil, to taste
red wine vinegar, to taste
sea salt and ground black pepper

This famous Tuscan salad has a substantial bread base with the addition of tomatoes, onions, cucumbers and basil to give it flavour and freshness. Served elegantly, in a pretty bowl or on a flat platter, this makes a wonderful appetizer. It is a rustic dish, perfect for hot summer days, and is a useful way of using up precious leftover bread, which needs to be coarse and crusty.

1 Soak the bread in cold water for about 15 minutes, then squeeze the bread dry in a clean dish towel.

2 Mix the damp bread with the tomatoes, onion, cucumber and basil.

3 Dress the salad with olive oil, vinegar and salt and pepper to taste.

4 Toss the salad ingredients together thoroughly and leave it to stand for about 30 minutes before serving.

COOK'S TIP
Extra virgin olive oil is a premium oil with a superior flavour and is perfect for tasty salad dressings.

Wild Boar Maltagliati in the Arezzo Style
Maltagliati al Sugo di Cinghiale all'Aretina

Serves 6

60ml/4 tbsp olive oil
1 onion, finely chopped
1 carrot, finely chopped
1 celery stick, finely chopped
115g/4oz prosciutto crudo, coarsely
   chopped
450g/1lb wild boar stewing meat,
   cubed
300ml/½ pint/1¼ cups full-bodied
   red wine
75ml/5 tbsp tomato purée (paste)
   diluted with 90ml/6 tbsp hot game
   or beef stock
275g/10oz canned tomatoes,
   strained
large pinch of fennel seeds
small pinch of ground cumin or
   cumin seed
450g/1lb maltagliati
sea salt and ground black pepper
freshly grated Parmesan cheese, to
   serve (optional)

1 Put the olive oil in a pan and fry the vegetables and prosciutto gently for 5 minutes, or until the onion is translucent.

2 Add the cubes of boar. Cook until browned all over, then pour over the wine and add seasoning. Cover and simmer for 1 hour.

3 Add half the diluted tomato purée and half the canned tomatoes to the meat and vegetable mixture. Cook for 1 hour more.

4 Add the remaining purée and tomatoes.

5 When the meat is falling apart, stir in the fennel seeds and cumin. Cover and simmer for a further 1 hour. Adjust the seasoning.

6 Bring a large pan of salted water to the boil, add the maltagliati, stir and then return to the boil. Cook according to the pack instructions, until al dente. Drain and return it to the pan.

7 Add the wild boar sauce to the pasta. Mix it through gently and transfer to a serving platter or individual plates to serve. Offer Parmesan cheese separately.

Tuscany can stake a claim to just two different pasta shapes: pappardelle and maltagliati. Neighbouring Emilia Romagna is the most important region in the entire country when it comes to fresh pasta and its traditions. In a gesture of typical Tuscan defiance, making pasta that is so obviously big and substantial is testament to the ongoing feuding between the two areas. Cinghiale (wild boar) is one of the most iconic of all the Tuscan specialities.

Serves 6

1.3kg/3lb fresh spinach
2 eggs, beaten
2 egg yolks
30ml/2 tbsp single (light) cream
150g/5oz stale bread, soaked in milk
    to cover for ½ hour
150g/5oz/1½ cups freshly grated
    Parmesan cheese
1.5ml/¼ tsp freshly grated nutmeg
up to 75ml/5 tbsp plain (all-purpose)
    flour
115g/4oz unsalted butter, melted
sea salt and ground black pepper

COOK'S TIP

Achieve lightness when shaping
the gnocchi, by rolling each ball
of dough around a glass tumbler,
dusted inside with flour. This
way, you will prevent the
gnocchi becoming too solid and
avoid squashing the air out.

Tuscan Spinach Gnocchi
Malfatti

1 Steam or boil the spinach for 1–2 minutes until soft. Drain and leave to cool. Squeeze out the water, then chop finely. Put the spinach in a large bowl and stir in the eggs and egg yolks, then the cream.

2 Squeeze the bread dry with your hands, then mix it into the spinach with half the Parmesan. Season to taste with nutmeg and salt and pepper. Bring a large pan of water to the boil.

3 Using your fingers and a very light touch (see Cook's Tip), form the mixture into small dumplings, using a small amount of flour to prevent sticking.

4 Transfer the dumplings carefully, in small batches, into the boiling water. Cook the gnocchi for no more than 2–3 minutes – they will be ready when they float freely on the surface of the water.

5 Carefully remove the cooked gnocchi from the water using a slotted spoon and arrange them on a warmed serving dish. Continue in this way, with the remaining batches, until all the gnocchi are cooked.

6 Smother the gnocchi with the melted butter, sprinkle over the remaining Parmesan cheese and serve immediately.

The word malfatti means 'badly made', so in other words they can look quite roughly shaped, without too much concern for elegant presentation. Malfatti are traditionally served simply with melted, warm, unsalted butter, but they can also be served with a basic tomato sauce. The recipe, in very similar versions, exists in various parts of the country, but this is the most classically Tuscan version.

Polenta and Beans Polenta e Fagioli

1 Rinse the soaked beans. Put them in a large pan and cover with plenty of water. Bring to the boil and boil hard for 5 minutes, then drain and rinse again. Return the beans to the pan, cover with fresh water, bring to the boil, and boil gently for 45 minutes, or until softened. Drain away most of the water.

2 In a separate pan, fry the lard, white cooking fat or pancetta with the carrot, celery and onion for 10 minutes, or until softened.

3 Add the tomatoes and stir together. Simmer until thickened and glossy, then season to taste.

4 Drain and add the boiled beans, stir to mix and simmer while you cook the polenta.

5 Bring 2 litres/3½ pints/9 cups water to the boil in a large pan. Add a large pinch of salt, then trickle the polenta flour into the boiling water in a steady stream, whisking constantly. Turn the heat to medium-low. Using a strong wooden spoon, stir the polenta constantly for about 40 minutes.

6 Add the beans and their sauce, reserving a little to serve, if you wish, and continue to stir and cook for a further 10 minutes. Serve sprinkled with Pecorino cheese and a drizzle of olive oil.

Polenta and beans, a peasant-food staple, is eaten all over Tuscany. This dish is made with standard polenta to which some beans, enriched with tomato sauce, are added. The incorporation of the stewed beans and their sauce into the polenta makes for a really tasty dish. It is traditionally served with a good sprinkling of freshly grated Pecorino cheese.

Serves 6

400g/14oz/2⅔ cups dried borlotti or cannellini beans, soaked overnight and drained

50g/2oz/⅓ cup lard, white cooking fat or fatty pancetta, cubed

1 carrot, finely chopped

1 celery stick, finely chopped

1 onion, finely chopped

450g/1lb ripe tomatoes, peeled, seeded and coarsely chopped

300g/11oz/2⅓ cups coarse or medium-grade polenta flour

sea salt and ground black pepper

freshly grated Pecorino cheese and extra virgin olive oil, to serve

Stuffed Sardines Sardine Ripiene

Serves 4

2–3 stale crusty white bread rolls, crusts removed

about 120ml/4fl oz/½ cup milk

40 fresh sardines or large anchovies, scaled and filleted

3 eggs, beaten

45ml/3 tbsp freshly grated Parmesan cheese

2 garlic cloves, chopped

30ml/1 tbsp tomato purée (paste)

a handful of fresh flat leaf parsley, leaves chopped

1 dried red chilli

about 90ml/6 tbsp plain (all-purpose) flour

about 2 litres/3½ pints/9 cups sunflower oil, for deep-frying

sea salt

This Tuscan recipe relies very much on the fish being freshly caught. Like many recipes from this region, the ingredients are quite generous and call for about ten fish per person. Serve just as they are, with a wedge of lemon.

1 Soak the bread in the milk to cover, then squeeze dry. Use any damaged fish fillets for the filling. Put all the perfectly shaped fillets to one side.

2 Mix the bread with the damaged fish, half the beaten eggs, the grated Parmesan cheese, garlic, tomato purée, parsley, chilli and a pinch of salt. Blend it all together to make a firm paste with your hands or a fork.

3 Sandwich two fillets together with a generous spoonful of the filling in the middle, then gently coat in the remaining beaten egg and then the flour. Repeat for the remaining fillets.

4 Heat the oil in large pan until sizzling, then fry the fish, in batches, until crisp and golden brown; about 2 minutes. Drain on kitchen paper and serve.

Marinated Eels Scaveccio

Serves 4

900g/2lb very fresh eels
coarse sea salt, for cleaning
150ml/¼ pint/⅔ cup extra virgin
   olive oil
3 garlic cloves
1 dried red chilli
3 fresh sage leaves
1 rosemary sprig
300ml/½ pint/1¼ cups white wine
   vinegar
sea salt

In the rivers and streams of the Tuscan plains, eels are caught and turned into delicious, simple dishes for the table. This is a very old recipe from the Pisa area, and is served cold as part of an antipasto. After 48 hours or so in the marinade, the strong, slightly muddy flavour of the eel is much reduced and the vinegar acts as a good foil to the natural oiliness of the fish.

1 Clean the outside of the eels carefully to remove all trace of slime, using coarse sea salt or gritty wood ash. Split and gut them carefully, then wash and dry them all over. Cut them into finger-length chunks.

2 Heat the oil in a frying pan and fry the eel chunks until golden brown all over. Remove them with a slotted spoon and drain on kitchen paper. Place in a bowl to cool.

3 Using the same oil, fry the garlic, chilli, sage and rosemary together for 3 minutes.

4 Add the white wine vinegar to the frying pan and then boil to reduce by about one-third. Season with salt.

5 Pour this marinade over the eels and cover the bowl. Leave to marinate for about 48 hours before serving.

Tuscan Fish Stew Cacciucco

Serves 6 to 8

1.8kg/4lb assorted fish in varying
 sizes, cleaned and gutted
450g/1lb octopus and squid, cleaned
150ml/¼ pint/⅔ cup virgin olive oil
1 onion, chopped
1 carrot, chopped
1 celery stick, chopped
a handful of fresh flat leaf parsley
 leaves, finely chopped
1 dried red chilli, finely chopped
4 garlic cloves, 3 chopped and 1
 halved
250ml/8fl oz/1 cup dry white wine
900g/2lb ripe tomatoes, peeled,
 seeded and coarsely chopped
12 large raw prawns (shrimp), peeled
 and deveined
15 small slices of crusty white bread
sea salt and ground black pepper
about 1 litre/1¾ pints/4 cups
 simmering fish or vegetable stock,
 for basting and diluting

*This classic fish stew, which
originates from the port of
Livorno, must contain at
least five varieties of fresh
fish, one for each of the 'C's
in the recipe's name.*

1 Cut the larger fish into generous pieces and leave the smaller ones whole. Keep all the heads, if removed, and set them aside. Cut the octopus and squid into large pieces.

2 Put the oil in a large frying pan and fry the onion, carrot, celery, parsley, chilli and chopped garlic for 10 minutes, or until lightly golden.

3 Add the octopus and squid to the pan and cook for 2–3 minutes, or until they have released their fluid and it has been evaporated. Pour over the white wine. Cook for 2 minutes, until the alcohol has evaporated, then add the tomatoes. Stir and cover.

4 Simmer for 45 minutes, or until the squid or octopus are tender, then remove them and set aside. Add the fish heads and smaller fish to the pan and stir. Cook for about 25 minutes, basting occasionally with a little hot water or stock.

5 Pass the sauce and fish through the medium blade of a food mill or mouli and return to the pan. You should have a smooth, thick sauce. If it is too thick, dilute with a little hot water or stock.

6 Add the larger whole fish and pieces of fish to the pan and stir gently to coat with the sauce. Simmer together very gently for about 20 minutes.

7 Return the octopus and squid to the pan, and stir into the sauce. Add the prawns and cover with sauce, using more of the stock if necessary. Cook for about 15 minutes, until all the seafood is tender.

8 Meanwhile, toast the bread and rub with the halved garlic clove. Line the sides of a large bowl with the toast.

9 Raise the heat under the pan and stir the fish and sauce together while it returns to the boil. Season to taste with salt and pepper. Immediately, remove the pan from the heat and transfer the cacciucco to the bowl lined with toasted bread. Serve immediately.

Salt Cod Fritters Frittelle di Baccalà

Serves 6

1.25kg/2¾lb salted cod, soaked for
  3 days, changing water frequently
1 egg
about 45ml/3 tbsp plain (all-purpose)
  flour
about 350ml/12fl oz/1½ cups cold
  water
about 2 litres/3½ pints/9 cups
  sunflower oil, for deep-frying

1 Drain the fish, pat dry with kitchen paper and remove any bones and skin. Cut into small fillets.

2 Mix together the egg, flour and enough water to make a thick coating batter. Use the batter to cover the fish completely.

3 Heat the oil until sizzling, then fry the fish in batches until golden brown.

4 Drain the fried fish on kitchen paper to remove the excess oil, then serve the fritters piping hot.

Although Tuscany has a coastline and many freshwater rivers, the ancient way of preserving fish in salt also has a place on the menu in this region, and these simple crispy fritters are a tasty way of eating salted cod.

COOK'S TIP

Try to buy fish that has already been soaked for three days to make sure that it has softened thoroughly, or you could soak it yourself, if you have the time.

Tuscan Rabbit Casserole
Coniglio alla Toscana

1 Put the rabbit joints into a bowl. Mix the wine vinegar with the water and pour over the rabbit. Soak for 1 hour.

2 Drain the rabbit joints and dry them carefully on kitchen paper. Chop half the garlic cloves and one rosemary sprig and mix them with the salt and pepper. Rub this mixture all over the rabbit joints.

3 Chop the remaining garlic. Heat the oil in a large pan and add the garlic and remaining rosemary. Fry the rabbit joints all over until brown. Add the red wine gradually, so that it simmers constantly.

4 Stir in the tomato purée and 300ml/½ pint/1¼ cups hot water. Cover and simmer gently for 45 minutes, or until cooked through. Serve.

COOK'S TIP
It is possible to buy rabbit jointed and ready for the pan.

Rabbit is a much-loved and respected meat in most parts of Italy, but perhaps especially in Tuscany, where every smallholding, farm or country home will have a few chickens and some rabbits kept for eating purposes in the back garden. Rabbit is lean and tasty, and at least 50 or so well-known recipes exist that are frequently and lovingly cooked. This is a truly ancient recipe, apparently dating back to the time of the Etruscans, and is a thoroughly tried-and-tested way of cooking rabbit, although the method also works with jointed chicken. Serve with polenta or roast potatoes.

Serves 8 to 10

2 rabbits, about 900g/2lb each, each cut into five pieces
90ml/6 tbsp strong red or white wine vinegar
600ml/1 pint/2½ cups water
6 garlic cloves, peeled
3 large rosemary sprigs
2.5ml/½ tsp sea salt
2.5ml/½ tsp ground black pepper
75ml/2½fl oz/⅓ cup olive oil
750ml/1¼ pints/3 cups red wine
15ml/1 tbsp tomato purée (paste)

Pork Sausages with Grapes
Salsicce all'uva

Serves 4
8 plump Italian sausages
10ml/2 tsp olive oil
30ml/2 tbsp water
8 handfuls firm grapes

1 Prick the sausages all over with a knife to allow the fat to run and the heat to permeate the sausage.

2 Put the oil and water in a large frying pan over a medium heat for 2 minutes.

3 Lay the sausages in the pan. Cook gently, turning frequently, for 10 minutes, or until cooked through.

4 Add the grapes. Cook until slightly caramelized, and then serve with roast potatoes and a green salad, if you like.

COOK'S TIP
Big, sweet, thick-skinned and firm, white grapes are best for this dish, however a mixture of white and red grapes will add colour.

In the early autumn, when grapes are plentiful, they taste delicious when fried in a pan with rich, pork sausages. If the pig has been recently killed for the celebration of a local festivity, as well as to put away cured meat for the cold winter ahead, the sausages will be fresh and tender.

Wild Boar Cacciatora Cinghiale alla Cacciatora

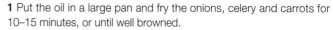

Serves 6

45ml/3 tbsp extra virgin olive oil
2 onions, thickly sliced
2 celery sticks, thickly sliced
2 carrots, thickly sliced
900g/2lb wild boar meat
about 500ml/17fl oz/2¼ cups dry red
   wine
1 large rosemary sprig
75ml/5 tbsp extra virgin olive oil
1 garlic clove, crushed
½ large onion, chopped
1 dried red chilli
300ml/½ pint/1¼ cups smooth
   passata
sea salt

1 Put the oil in a large pan and fry the onions, celery and carrots for 10–15 minutes, or until well browned.

2 Meanwhile, cut the wild boar into large chunks and place in a deep bowl. Pour in the wine and add the rosemary and then the vegetables. The wine should cover the meat completely; add more wine if necessary and mix everything together with your hands. Leave the meat to marinate overnight.

3 Drain and dry the meat, reserving the marinade. In a wide, preferably non-stick, pan, brown all the meat so that it releases its juices.

4 Once the meat has released its liquid, remove and set it aside. Discard the liquid left in the pan.

5 To make the cacciatora sauce, add the oil to the pan with the garlic, onion and chilli. Fry together for 5 minutes, stirring, then pour over the passata. Season with salt and simmer gently for 10 minutes.

6 Add the meat to the sauce. Lower the heat, cover and simmer, stirring occasionally, for 1 hour, or until tender. Add some more of the marinade if the meat appears to be drying out while simmering. Serve with spinach, if you like.

Cinghiale, or wild boar, is synonymous with Tuscan cuisine. In the forests and mountains of the entire region, this wild animal has long been prized for its excellent meat. The cooking time for the meat will largely depend upon the age of the wild boar. The older the animal, the longer the cooking time. Serve with greens, such as spinach.

Tuscan Pot Roast Stracotto alla Toscana

1 Pierce the meat all over with the point of a sharp knife and insert strips of garlic to taste, depending on how much you like garlic or the size of the cloves.

2 Put a large flameproof casserole over medium heat and add the pancetta, butter, onion, carrot and celery. Fry together for about 8 minutes, stirring constantly.

3 Add the meat and seal it on all sides.

4 Pour over about 300ml/½ pint/1¼ cups stock, season with salt and pepper and stir in the tomato purée.

5 Cover and simmer over a very low heat for about 6 hours, adding more stock occasionally to prevent the casserole from drying out.

6 When the meat is tender and cooked through, remove it from the casserole and set it aside to keep warm.

7 Rub the vegetables and stock left in the casserole through a sieve, strainer or food mill, and season to taste.

8 Slice the meat thickly and arrange it on a warmed platter. Pour over the sieved sauce and serve.

Serves 4

1.5kg/3¼lb beef brisket in a single piece
2–3 garlic cloves, cut into long strips
50g/2oz fatty pancetta, chopped
75g/3oz/6 tbsp unsalted butter
1 onion, chopped
1 carrot, chopped
1 celery stick, chopped
1 litre/1¾ pints/4 cups simmering beef stock
15ml/1 tbsp tomato purée (paste)
sea salt and ground black pepper

This hearty pot roast is delicious served with plenty of red wine, and is often brought to the table with polenta or mashed potatoes as an accompaniment. It is cooked over an extremely low heat for about 6 hours, which gives wonderfully tender beef and a rich stock with which to make a thick and tasty sauce.

Wild Mushroom Salad
Insalata di Funghi crudi

Serves 4

500g/1¼lb mixed wild or cultivated
    mushrooms
200g/7oz Parmesan cheese
a large handful of fresh flat leaf
    parsley leaves, finely chopped
juice of ½ lemon
extra virgin olive oil, to drizzle
sea salt and ground black pepper

1 Clean and trim the mushrooms carefully. Do not wash them, but use a brush to clean off any traces of soil.

2 Once clean, slice the mushrooms very thinly. Shave the Parmesan as thinly as possible.

3 Arrange the sliced mushrooms on a large platter, then sprinkle the chopped parsley and Parmesan shavings over the top.

4 Sprinkle with lemon juice, drizzle with oil and season. Serve within half an hour.

COOK'S TIPS

• Choose a mildly flavoured olive oil for drizzling over this salad, so that you do not overpower the mushrooms.

• Serve this dish within 30 minutes so that the mushrooms don't dry up.

This delicately flavoured salad makes the most of the special taste of raw mushrooms, and is traditionally made using fresh porcini or other wild mushrooms. You can also make the salad using cultivated or field mushrooms, but remember to slice them as thinly as possible.

The Flag
La Bandiera

Serves 4

450g/1lb ripe tomatoes
45ml/3 tbsp extra virgin olive oil
1 onion, sliced
450g/1lb red (bell) peppers, seeded
    and sliced
sea salt

This pepper stew is almost a purée by the time it has been cooked gently for almost 40 minutes, but it is really delicious either as a side dish with meat or as part of an antipasto. It can even be added to beaten eggs and turned into the most flavoursome frittata, and is also good with cheese. The name of the dish is thought to refer to the brightness of the colour.

1 First, peel the tomatoes. Place the tomatoes in a large heatproof bowl and cover with boiling water. Leave for 30 seconds, then carefully drain them. Prickk the sking with a sharp knife and the skins should peel off easily. Chop the flesh, discarding the seeds.

2 Put the oil in a pan and fry the onion for 5 minutes, or until softened but not browned.

3 Add the sliced peppers, stir, and cook for 10 minutes.

4 Add the chopped tomatoes, season with salt and stir well. Simmer the mixture gently, stirring frequently, for about 30 minutes, or until the peppers and tomatoes have softened completely.

Green Beans in the Florentine Style
Fagiolini alla Fiorentina

Serves 4

7.5ml/1½ tsp fennel seeds
450g/1lb green beans, trimmed
75ml/5 tbsp olive oil
1 large red onion, thinly sliced
20ml/4 tsp tomato purée (paste)
   diluted in 60ml/4 tbsp hot water
sea salt and ground black pepper

1 Crush the fennel seeds to a powder in a spice grinder or using a mortar and pestle.

2 Boil the beans in a pan of lightly salted water until tender.

3 Meanwhile, heat the oil in a large frying pan, add the onion and fry until soft.

4 Stir in the diluted tomato purée and the crushed fennel seeds.

5 Drain the beans thoroughly and toss them into the pan. Mix well and season to taste.

6 Cover and cook through for 10–15 minutes more, then serve.

This is a sure-fire way to liven up green beans. Even frozen green beans, which are rarely tasty, take on a new lease of life. For this dish, Florentine cooks use the dried fennel seed that is so popular in local recipes. The beans are allowed to cook until they are really soft and have absorbed as much as possible of the surrounding flavours.

Stewed Beans
Fagioli All'Uccelletto

Serves 4

45–60ml/3–4 tbsp olive oil
3 cloves garlic, peeled and crushed
2 or 3 leaves fresh sage
400g/14oz can cannellini beans, drained
200g/7oz canned tomatoes, strained
sea salt and ground black pepper

1 Put the oil in a pan and gently fry the garlic and sage.

2 When the oil is golden brown, add the beans and season with a pinch of ground black pepper.

3 Stir the mixture together thoroughly, then add the strained tomatoes. Simmer gently for a further 20 minutes.

4 Check and adjust the seasoning to taste, then serve.

COOK'S TIP
• If using dried beans, soak them overnight in cold water, boil hard in fresh water for 5 minutes, then rinse and use as fresh.
• This dish can also be made using rosemary instead of sage, though the sage gives a more subtle flavour.

Tuscans love their beans, and this recipe is a real classic. Delicious hot or cold, it can be served on its own or as part of another dish, for example on top of toasted bread as crostini or alongside meat or fish dishes. It is a very adaptable recipe that can be made with canned or dried beans, or fresh beans when they are in season.

Deep-fried Courgettes Zucchini Fritti

1 Cut the courgettes into thin strips with a potato peeler or mandolin.

2 In a bowl, beat together the egg yolk, flour and milk, or mixed milk and water, to make a smooth paste. Put the egg white into a clean, grease-free bowl and whisk until stiff. Gently fold into the batter.

3 Carefully dip the courgettes into the batter to coat thoroughly.

4 Heat the oil in a wide, deep pan until a small cube of bread dropped into it sizzles instantly.

5 Carefully lower the courgette strips into the hot oil and deep-fry for 4 minutes, or until crisp and golden all over, turning frequently. (If they take longer than this the oil is not hot enough.)

6 Drain thoroughly on kitchen paper, sprinkle with a little salt and serve immediately.

VARIATIONS

If using courgette flowers, you could try filling them before frying.
• For a punchy flavour, push a small piece of anchovy and a cube of mozzarella cheese into the centre of the flower.
• For a smooth, sweet taste that contrasts brilliantly with the crispy fried flower, use a spoonful of ricotta cheese.

Serves 4
2 courgettes (zucchini)
1 egg, separated
40g/1½oz/⅓ cup plain (all-purpose) flour
150ml/¼ pint/⅔ cup milk, or milk mixed with water
600ml/1 pint/2½ cups sunflower oil, for deep-frying
sea salt

This Tuscan delicacy can be made with courgette flowers, if they are available, but using thin slices of courgette is much simpler and tastes delicious. If you do choose to use flowers, check them on the inside for insects before proceeding, and remove the pistil, which will taste bitter.

Tuscan Grape-harvest Focaccia
Schiacciata D'uva

Makes 6

extra olive oil, for greasing
semolina or polenta flour, for dusting
35g/1¼ oz fresh yeast
300ml/¼ pint/1¼ cups warm water
pinch of sugar
450g/1lb/4 cups strong white bread
   flour, plus extra for dusting
5ml/1 tsp sea salt
15ml/3 tsp extra olive oil, plus extra
   for greasing
plain (all-purpose) flour, for dusting
450g/1lb fresh black or white
   grapes, seedless
15–30ml/1–2 tbsp caster (superfine)
   sugar

This type of sweet bread is made around the time of the wine harvest – vendemmia – when there is a bountiful supply of fresh, sweet grapes around.

1 Preheat the oven to 220°C/425°F/Gas 7. Oil two baking sheets generously and dust with semolina or polenta flour.

2 Make the bread dough. Mix the yeast and water together in a small bowl. Add the sugar and 30ml/2 tbsp of the flour. Leave in a warm place for about 30 minutes, or until it becomes frothy.

3 Put the remaining flour on to the work surface. Make a well in the centre of the flour and pour in the yeast mixture. Work the yeast mixture into the flour, then add the salt and the oil and knead for 10 minutes, or until the dough becomes soft and elastic.

4 Transfer the dough to a large floured bowl, cover with lightly oiled clear film (plastic wrap) and leave to rise in a warm place for 2 hours, or until doubled in size.

5 Divide the dough into six portions. On a floured work surface, roll them into 1cm/½ in thick circles and place on the baking sheets.

6 Drizzle the surface of each schiacciata with a little oil, then cover each one with grapes.

7 Press the grapes down into the dough with the flat of your hand. Sprinkle with the sugar and bake for 15–20 minutes, or until cooked through. Serve warm or cold.

COOK'S TIPS
• You need to squash the grapes down well into the top of the focaccia base, using plenty of sugar to bring out the flavour of the ripe fruit.
• The amount of sugar you need will depend on the sweetness of the grapes.

Tuscan Hard Dunking Cookies Cantucci

1 Preheat the oven to 150°C/300°F/Gas 2. Oil two baking sheets.

2 Lay the almonds out on a baking sheet and toast them under a hot grill (broiler), turning occasionally, for about 5 minutes, or until golden. Chop coarsely.

3 Put the flour on to a work surface and use your fist to make a hollow in the centre. Pour the eggs into the hollow. Add the sugar, ammonium carbonate or bicarbonate of soda, and salt. Mix together, then add the almonds.

4 Knead everything together thoroughly and shape the dough with your hands into several thick strips about 7.5cm/3in long, 6cm/2½in wide and 2.5cm/1in thick.

5 Slide the strips of dough on to the baking sheets and bake in the preheated oven for 10 minutes, or until golden.

6 Cut the strips into cookie-sized lengths, on the diagonal. Return them to the oven for a further 6 minutes, to crisp them.

7 Cool the cookies on a wire rack. Store in an airtight container for up to three months.

COOK'S TIP
The traditional raising agent is ammonium carbonate, but it is sometimes difficult to obtain. Bicarbonate of soda (baking soda) will also work.

Italians love to dunk, and these cookies are made for being dunked into a glass of Vinsanto, Tuscany's favourite sweet dessert wine, or a cup of dark and fragrant espresso coffee. They make a simple but very satisfying sweet snack at any time.

Serves 8 to 10

oil, for greasing
225g/8oz/1⅓ cups blanched
    almonds
1kg/2¼lb plain (all-purpose) flour,
    sifted
8 eggs, beaten
1kg/2¼lb/generous 5 cups caster
    (superfine) sugar
10ml/2 tsp ammonium carbonate
    (see Cook's Tip)
pinch of salt

Makes 1 cake

150g/5oz/⅔ cup short grain rice
1.2 litres/2 pints/5 cups milk
butter, for greasing
30ml/2 tbsp semolina
9 eggs
225g/8oz/generous 1 cup caster
  (superfine) sugar
45ml/3 tbsp brandy
grated rind of 1 unwaxed lemon

Soft Tuscan Rice Cake
La torta Di Riso

1 Put the rice and 750ml/1¼ pints/3 cups of the milk into a pan. Boil for 10 minutes, then drain, reserving the milk, which will have absorbed some of the starch from the rice. Set aside to cool slightly.

2 Preheat the oven to 180°C/350°F/Gas 4. Butter a 25cm/10in fixed-base cake tin or pan, thoroughly, and then sprinkle with the semolina. (Do not use a loose-based tin, or all the liquid will leak.) Turn the cake tin upside down and shake gently to remove any loose semolina.

3 Using an electric whisk, beat the eggs in a large bowl until foaming and pale yellow. Add the sugar gradually, beating constantly, then add the brandy and lemon rind. Stir well.

4 Add the rice and remaining milk (including the reserved milk). Pour into the cake tin.

5 Bake for 50 minutes, or until a cocktail stick (toothpick) inserted into the centre comes out clean. The cake should be well set and golden brown. Serve warm or cold.

COOK'S TIP
Don't worry about how runny the mixture seems when you pour it into the tin or pan; the finished cake should remain very moist and sticky when baked, and just be firm enough to slice neatly into portions.

It is the rich, eggy and sticky quality of this cake that makes it the traditional Tuscan children's cake – despite containing a little brandy. Delicious and incredibly filling, it is like a home-made version of those little oval rice cakes you can buy at all Tuscan cafés and pâtisseries, called simply budino, which literally translates as 'pudding'. This is the classic version of the recipe, but you can vary the cake by adding nuts or candied fruits, if you like.

Tuscan Candied Fruit-and-nut Hard Cake
Panforte

Makes 1 cake

rice paper
200g/7oz/generous 1 cup
    unblanched almonds
225g/8oz/1 cup mixed (candied)
    peel, chopped
50g/2oz/¼ cup crystallized (candied)
    orange peel
130g/4½oz/generous ⅔ cup shelled
    walnuts
200g/7oz/1¾ cups plain (all-
    purpose) flour
5ml/1 tsp ground cinnamon
2.5ml/½ tsp ground allspice
2.5ml/½ tsp ground coriander
350g/12oz/1¾ cups caster
    (superfine) sugar
30ml/2 tbsp clear honey
15ml/1 tbsp each ground cinnamon
    and icing (confectioners') sugar,
    sifted together, for dusting

*Panforte is an old-fashioned
sweetmeat, which dates
back to the Renaissance
and was reputedly first
created in Siena. Serve in
narrow strips.*

1 Preheat the oven to 150°C/300°F/Gas 2 and line a 25cm/10in round shallow cake tin or pan with rice paper or baking parchment.

2 Blanch 150g/5oz almonds by soaking them in hot water for about 1 minute, then removing the skins.

3 Lay the blanched almonds out on a baking sheet and toast them under a hot grill (broiler), turning occasionally, for about 5 minutes, or until golden. Chop them coarsely.

4 Put the chopped almonds into a food processor or blender with the chopped mixed peel, the crystallized orange peel and the walnuts. Whiz until it forms a rough mass. (Alternatively, chop very finely using a sharp knife.) Put the mixture on to a work surface.

5 Combine the nut and peel mixture with the remaining unblanched almonds and the flour and spices.

6 In a small pan, melt the sugar and honey together and boil until it reaches the 'soft ball stage' (119°C/238°F; see the Cook's Tip). Pour the hot sugar and honey mixture over the dry ingredients and mix well with a spatula and, when cooler, using your hands.

7 Press the mixture into the tin. Level in the tin using a spatula and bake in the oven for 30 minutes, or until golden.

8 Remove the cake from the oven and allow to cool on a wire rack. Dust with the icing sugar and cinnamon mixture.

COOK'S TIP
You can use a sugar thermometer to measure the temperature of the sugar accurately. However, you can always use the other method: drop a tiny amount into a small cup of cold water. It is ready if it forms a perfect ball when you roll it between your thumb and index finger.

Soft Almond Sweetmeats | Ricciarelli

Makes about 12

200g/7oz/generous 1 cup blanched
    almonds
115g/4oz/⅔ cup pine nuts
200g/7oz/1 cup caster (superfine)
    sugar
5ml/1 tsp vanilla extract
2 egg whites
grated rind of ½ small unwaxed
    orange
115g/4oz/1 cup icing (confectioners')
    sugar, sifted

*These delicately flavoured
Tuscan soft almond
sweetmeats are traditionally
eaten at Christmas time.
The bought versions are
perfectly shaped, like large
lozenges, and pure white in
colour. This recipe for
home-made ricciarelli gives
you a less aesthetically
faultless result, but is
delicious nonetheless.*

1 Pound the almonds and the pine nuts together to make a fine powder using a mortar and pestle, or alternatively, pulse in a food processor.

2 Transfer into a bowl and add the caster sugar and vanilla extract. Mix thoroughly.

3 Put the egg whites into a clean, grease-free bowl and whisk into stiff peaks form.

4 Carefully fold the grated orange rind into the egg whites, then fold in the almond mixture.

5 Line a baking sheet with baking parchment, then put heaped tablespoonfuls of the mixture on to the parchment, set well apart. Chill for about 6 hours.

6 Preheat the oven to 150°C/300°F/Gas 2. Bake the sweetmeats for 15 minutes. Cool on a wire rack and sprinkle generously with the icing sugar before serving.

Nutritional notes

Tuscan Cold Summer Soup: Energy 119kcal/494kJ; Protein 1.3g; Carbohydrate 7.2g, of which sugars 6.9g; Fat 9.7g, of which saturates 1.4g; Cholesterol 0mg; Calcium 33mg; Fibre 2.9g; Sodium 23mg.

Tomato and Bread Soup: Energy 285kcal/1194kJ; Protein 5g; Carbohydrate 28g, of which sugars 7.2g; Fat 17.9g, of which saturates 2.5g; Cholesterol 0mg; Calcium 64mg; Fibre 2.6g; Sodium 243mg.

Tuscan Bean, Sausage and Cabbage Soup: Energy 354kcal/1482kJ; Protein 11.5g; Carbohydrate 43.8g, of which sugars 12g; Fat 15.9g, of which saturates 4.9g; Cholesterol 16mg; Calcium 151mg; Fibre 5.8g; Sodium 617mg.

Tuscan Bread Fritters: Energy 604kcal/2518kJ; Protein 9.3g; Carbohydrate 58.5g, of which sugars 1.1g; Fat 38.5g, of which saturates 5.4g; Cholesterol 0mg; Calcium 110mg; Fibre 2.3g; Sodium 6mg.

Tuscan Liver Pâté: Energy 472kcal/1979kJ; Protein 16.6g; Carbohydrate 48.7g, of which sugars 4.8g; Fat 23.8g, of which saturates 8.3g; Cholesterol 177mg; Calcium 124mg; Fibre 2.2g; Sodium 596mg.

Tuscan Bread and Tomato Salad: Energy 238kcal/998kJ; Protein 5.3g; Carbohydrate 28g, of which sugars 5.9g; Fat 12.5g, of which saturates 1.9g; Cholesterol 0mg; Calcium 116mg; Fibre 3.2g; Sodium 259mg.

Wild Boar Maltagliati in the Arezzo Style: Energy 539kcal/2268kJ; Protein 30.8g; Carbohydrate 62.2g, of which sugars 8.7g; Fat 16.6g, of which saturates 4.3g; Cholesterol 55mg; Calcium 49mg; Fibre 3.9g; Sodium 327mg.

Tuscan Spinach Gnocchi: Energy 465kcal/1933kJ; Protein 22.5g; Carbohydrate 25.7g, of which sugars 4.3g; Fat 30.8g, of which saturates 17.5g; Cholesterol 202mg; Calcium 738mg; Fibre 5.3g; Sodium 879mg.

Polenta and Beans: Energy 458kcal/1926kJ; Protein 20.2g; Carbohydrate 70.4g, of which sugars 5.8g; Fat 11.1g, of which saturates 3.6g; Cholesterol 8mg; Calcium 82mg; Fibre 12.9g; Sodium 26mg.

Stuffed Sardines: Energy 621kcal/2594kJ; Protein 35.8g; Carbohydrate 37.2g, of which sugars 2.6g; Fat 37.7g, of which saturates 9.3g; Cholesterol 155mg; Calcium 343mg; Fibre 1.3g; Sodium 505mg.

Marinated Eels: Energy 603kcal/2499kJ; Protein 37.4g; Carbohydrate 0g, of which sugars 0g; Fat 50.4g, of which saturates 10g; Cholesterol 338mg; Calcium 43mg; Fibre 0g; Sodium 200mg.

Tuscan Fish Stew: Energy 585kcal/2458kJ; Protein 52.9g; Carbohydrate 46.8g, of which sugars 6.5g; Fat 19.8g, of which saturates 3.2g; Cholesterol 92mg; Calcium 168mg; Fibre 2.7g; Sodium 657mg.

Salt Cod Fritters: Energy 429kcal/1786kJ; Protein 39.9g; Carbohydrate 5.8g, of which sugars 0.1g; Fat 27.5g, of which saturates 3.1g; Cholesterol 128mg; Calcium 34mg; Fibre 0.2g; Sodium 137mg.

Tuscan Rabbit Casserole: Energy 265kcal/1106kJ; Protein 25.2g; Carbohydrate 0.4g, of which sugars 0.4g; Fat 12.5g, of which saturates 3.7g; Cholesterol 124mg; Calcium 17mg; Fibre 0g; Sodium 40mg.

Pork Sausages with Grapes: Energy 638kcal/2648kJ; Protein 16.3g; Carbohydrate 29.7g, of which sugars 17.5g; Fat 51.3g, of which saturates 18.7g; Cholesterol 71mg; Calcium 75mg; Fibre 1.5g; Sodium 1142mg.

Wild Boar Cacciatora: Energy 430kcal/1791kJ; Protein 33.8g; Carbohydrate 7.5g, of which sugars 4.7g; Fat 23.5g, of which saturates 5.1g; Cholesterol 100mg; Calcium 39mg; Fibre 1.5g; Sodium 294mg.

Tuscan Pot Roast: Energy 707kcal/2955kJ; Protein 81.7g; Carbohydrate 2.7g, of which sugars 2.3g; Fat 41.2g, of which saturates 20.6g; Cholesterol 254mg; Calcium 30mg; Fibre 0.7g; Sodium 537mg.

Wild Mushroom Salad: Energy 247kcal/1027kJ; Protein 22.3g; Carbohydrate 0.9g, of which sugars 0.5g; Fat 17.2g, of which saturates 10.4g; Cholesterol 50mg; Calcium 633mg; Fibre 2g; Sodium 556mg.

The Flag: Energy 129kcal/538kJ; Protein 1.9g; Carbohydrate 10.7g, of which sugars 10.4g; Fat 9g, of which saturates 1.4g; Cholesterol 0mg; Calcium 17mg; Fibre 2.9g; Sodium 15mg.

Green Beans in the Florentine Style: Energy 181kcal/747kJ; Protein 3.3g; Carbohydrate 10.2g, of which sugars 7.4g; Fat 14.5g, of which saturates 2.1g; Cholesterol 0mg; Calcium 62mg; Fibre 3.7g; Sodium 14mg.

Stewed Beans: Energy 160kcal/669kJ; Protein 6.3g; Carbohydrate 14.6g, of which sugars 2.7g; Fat 8.9g, of which saturates 1.3g; Cholesterol 0mg; Calcium 19mg; Fibre 5.1g; Sodium 425mg.

Deep-fried Courgettes: Energy 187kcal/774kJ; Protein 5.4g; Carbohydrate 11.5g, of which sugars 3.7g; Fat 13.5g, of which saturates 2.2g; Cholesterol 53mg; Calcium 90mg; Fibre 1.2g; Sodium 40mg.

Tuscan Grape-harvest Focaccia: Energy 337kcal/1432kJ; Protein 7.4g; Carbohydrate 75.1g, of which sugars 17.9g; Fat 2.9g, of which saturates 0.3g; Cholesterol 0mg; Calcium 117mg; Fibre 2.9g; Sodium 4mg.

Tuscan Hard Dunking Cookies: Energy 932kcal/3946kJ; Protein 19.7g; Carbohydrate 183.8g, of which sugars 107g; Fat 18.3g, of which saturates 2.5g; Cholesterol 152mg; Calcium 270mg; Fibre 4.8g; Sodium 68mg.

Soft Tuscan Rice Cake: Energy 2838kcal/11969kJ; Protein 111.3g; Carbohydrate 438.1g, of which sugars 295.1g; Fat 71.6g, of which saturates 25.9g; Cholesterol 1783mg; Calcium 1850mg; Fibre 0.6g; Sodium 1307mg.

Tuscan Candied Fruit-and-nut Hard Cake: Energy 9564kcal/40476kJ; Protein 91g; Carbohydrate 1911.9g, of which sugars 1748g; Fat 225.7g, of which saturates 17.4g; Cholesterol 0mg; Calcium 4054mg; Fibre 134.8g; Sodium 6443mg.

Soft Almond Sweetmeats: Energy 273kcal/1144kJ; Protein 5.5g; Carbohydrate 29g, of which sugars 28.5g; Fat 15.9g, of which saturates 1.2g; Cholesterol 0mg; Calcium 55mg; Fibre 1.4g; Sodium 14mg.

Index